T.—By no means. There are honorable and exemplary exceptions.

P.—Have the Travelling Preachers, then, no opportunity of conversing with the members of the church individually?

T.—By the laws of Methodism, and by their temporal wants, they are compelled to see every member, at what is called the *Quarterly Visitation*.

P.—Perhaps this supersedes the necessity of pastoral visits of another kind?

T.—Judge for yourself. At the Quarterly Visitation a single Preacher will write the names of a hundred members on as many Society tickets; receive the shilling, or upwards, subscribed for their support from each; and *closely* converse with the same number of persons upon their spiritual state. All this in the space of perhaps two hours or less.

P.—His expedition is commendable, certainly.

T.—Yes. But what becomes of his fidelity? That is the question.

P.—What reason is assigned for the neglect of this most important part of a minister's duty?

T.—For not visiting the *schools*, a multiplicity of Conference business has been assigned as an excuse. Perhaps it may serve for both.

P.—" What is the office of a Christian minister?

T.—" To watch over souls, as he that must give an account.

P.—" What does St. James mean by 'respect of persons?'

T.—" The regarding one person more than another, on account of some outward circumstances, particularly riches.

P.—" Have they not fallen into this by spending more time with the rich than with the poor, and by not speaking so plain and home to them?"*

* John Wesley,—vide " Myles' Chron. Hist." p. 94.

T.—Most notoriously they have; when they ought to " visit the people from house to house, exhort them to walk closely with God, and to be diligent in meeting the *children* every week."*

P.—Do not the people complain of this neglect?

T.—Their complaints are frequent and heartrending, but fruitless; though they be often the complaints of the aged, the infirm, the unfortunate, and the dying saint; to say nothing of the rest.

SECTION III.

LOCAL PREACHERS.

Pupil.—What is a Local Preacher?

Tutor.—One who confesses himself called, or inwardly moved, by the Holy Ghost to preach the Gospel; and, whose qualifications being approved by his brethren, is by the church set apart to the office and work of the ministry.

P.—What is the difference between a Local and a Travelling Preacher?

T.—The one is sent out by the church alone, the other by the Conference also.

P.—Are not both acknowledged to be ministers of the Gospel?

T.—Evidently so.

P.—Is there no other difference between a Travelling and a Local Preacher?

T.—Yes. The former is supported by the people; the latter supports himself.

P.—Is this difference to be considered in the favour of the Local Preacher, or against him?

T.—In his favour, certainly, if St. Paul's boasting had any just grounds.

* John Wesley,—vide "Myles' Chron. Hist." p. 125.

P.—Have not some Travelling Preachers insinuated that the difference is in *their* favour?

T.—Yes: a Mr. Beecham has said so, and many of the Travelling Preachers think so. But the idea is ridiculously preposterous.

P.—Where do the Local Preachers exercise their ministerial duties?

T.—In general they are excluded from the pulpits of the large towns; and, preaching where Christ has not been named, they extend the boundaries of the church, form new congregations, and, the way being thus smoothed as by a pioneer, the Travelling Preacher enters comfortably into their labours.

P.—Have not the distinctive characters of the Local Preacher and the Travelling Preacher changed places of late years?

T.—Yes. The Local Preacher is now made to travel, and the Travelling Preacher has become local, or stationary.

P.—Who pays the travelling expenses of the Local Preacher?

T.—Himself, in general, or he travels afoot.

P.—Is there not, on the part of some of the Travelling Preachers, a strong disposition to disparage the labours of their Local brethren?

T.—In their official capacity they are often treated with as much contempt as a wealthy pluralist in the Establishment sometimes shows to a poor curate.

P.—But is there no difference between the poor curate and the Local Preacher?

T.—Yes. The former receives £50 per annum for his services; the latter nothing.

P.—Then I am to understand that in Methodism the ministerial office is not exclusively held by the Travelling Preacher?

T.—Certainly not. It is divided between him, the Local Preacher, and the Class Leader. To one is assigned the *extension*, to a second the *over-sight*, and to a third, in a certain sense, the *building up* of the church.

P.—I presume, then, that the *government* of the church will not be exclusively held by the Travelling Preacher?

T.—The Lord judge between them. In justice it cannot be.

P.—Why?

T.—Because the same reason on which the Travelling Preacher claims it, demands it also for the Leader and the Local Preacher; for the ministerial office being divided amongst the three, the power attached thereto must be divided also.

P.—You have shown, from the nature of the case, that the ministerial power ought to be divided; but do the laws of Methodism sanction this division?

T.—Yes. Hear the voice of Conference on this subject, in their Concessions of 1797:—" Thus, brethren, we have given up the *greatest part* of our executive government into your hands."

P.—Is there any probability that the order of men amongst us called Local Preachers will eventually become extinct?

T.—Let them look to themselves. The jealousy of the Preachers, and the superciliousness of some worldly-minded, but ruling members of our congregations, would soon bring this about. The projected college was, probably, to have assisted in their overthrow. This, however, is certain, that Methodism may exist without the Travelling, but it cannot without the Local Preachers. There is no class of men in our communion more useful, or more important, and none more neglected.

SECTION IV.

LEADERS' MEETINGS.

Pupil.—What is a Leaders' Meeting?

Tutor.—A meeting composed of the Leaders in that division of a circuit which is attached to a particular chapel, the business of which consists in paying in to the Steward the peoples' penny a week, subscribed for the Preachers' support.

P.—Has it not also a judicial character?

T.—Yes. Leaders, as well as private members, being accused of any breach of the laws of Methodism, are entitled to a trial before such meeting, and can only be expelled the Society in consequence of a verdict of the majority of such meeting.

P.—Has not the Superintendent Preacher some authority in such trial?

T.—None at all. He has simply to pronounce the sentence of the law, when authorized to do so by the majority of the meeting.

P.—What is the law of the case in question?

T.—In regard to private members it runs thus,— "No person must be expelled from the Society for any breach of our rules, or even for manifest immorality, till such fact or crime has been proved at a Leaders' Meeting." (See Rules of Society, sec. 2.)

P.—Have not some preachers attempted to evade this law in some way?

T.—Yes; by a mere quibble. They say the law requires simply that the alleged crime be proved *in the presence,* not to the *satisfaction,* of the Leaders' Meeting.

P.—But such could not have been the construction put upon the law by our jealous forefathers when it was originally proposed to them?

T.—Certainly not. They must have seen that with such an interpretation the law was no protection to them : they must, therefore, have understood it as requiring that the crime be proved to the *satisfaction* of the whole, or, at least, of the majority of the Leaders. With any other explanation the trial is an absurdity, and might as well have taken place, without a jury of Leaders, in the Preacher's parlour.

P.—But, has not the popular construction of the rule been admitted by the Conference party ?

T.—It has. Mr. Watson (page 3 of his Affectionate Address) says, "The Constitution provides that *no person* shall be expelled from Society, or be removed from office, but *in conjunction* with the Leaders' Meeting." The "Methodist Magazine" for May, 1829, also interprets the phrase, "*at* a Leaders' Meeting," as meaning, "*to the satisfaction* of such meeting."

P.—What is the law with regard to a Leader ?

T.—"No person shall be appointed a Leader, or be removed from office, but in conjunction with the Leaders' Meeting ; the nomination to be in the Superintendent, and the approbation or disapprobation to be in the Leaders' Meeting." (Concessions, sec. 4.)

P.—Have the laws relative to expulsions ever been violated by the Preachers ?

T.—Nothing more common.

P.—Mention some instances.

T.—From the allusion to clandestine expulsions in the Concessions of 1797, it would appear that such things have been an old grievance.

P.—But have there been no modern cases ?

T.—Its privileges were invaded, in the Leeds case, by Messrs. Bunting and Newton, and about twenty other Travelling Preachers, who, without sanction of law, entered and overawed a Leaders' Meeting, with the view of inducing the protesting Leaders to sign a Preachers' party document, which being refused to be done, a resolution was proposed, that those who so refused should be expelled from office; by which means about twelve Leaders, who were present, and from twenty to thirty, who were absent, were, contrary to the laws and usages of Methodism, expelled without a trial ! !*

P.—Are there any recent instances of a similar kind ?

T.—Yes. The expulsion of Mr. John Greenhalgh, of Manchester, for the *crime* of being an advocate of the Association. Mr. Greenhalgh had been a man of eminent respectability as a Member of Society for twenty years; of which he had been a Class-leader, and a Local Preacher, seventeen years, and was also a Trustee. Also, by the expulsion, upon the same charge, of Mr. David Rowland, of Liverpool, than whom a more estimable and useful individual does not exist in connexion with the Society there. Mr. Rowland had been a Member of Society thirty years, an exceedingly popular Local Preacher twenty-two years, and a Leader twenty years, with a class of nearly sixty members.

P.—Have you any further instances to mention ?

T.—Yes; and of a more audacious character. The Superintendent Preacher, at the same time that he pronounced the unjust sentence of excommunication upon Mr. Rowland, declared, upon his own authority, without even asking the sanction of the meeting, four other estimable brethren to be no longer members of Society.

P.—Have not some persons been induced to leave the Society, in consequence of the Preachers' unjustifiable behaviour, in other ways ?

* Vide Address of the Protesting Leaders, &c.

T.—Yes: by their arbitrary conduct and insulting speeches, which honest men cannot bear. The number of excellent individuals thus driven away, in bitterness of soul, is as revolting as it is incredible. Thank God, that, by means of the Association, a remedy has at length been discovered.

P.—What can the Leaders have been about to permit such a flagrant invasion of their rights?

T.—They are, perhaps, piously reminded by the Preacher how becoming it would be to study the laws less and their Bibles more; and they, of course, not suspecting the manœuvre, sit down in ignorance, and the Preachers act with impunity.

P.—How may such arbitrary proceedings be checked?

T.—Only by the Leaders, in their official meetings, obliging every brother to be acquainted with the laws before they admit him amongst them.

P.—But, suppose the Preachers should persevere, notwithstanding?

T.—Then they must use their legal prerogative, and summon the meeting, appointed by the law in such case, to try the transgressing Preacher.

P.—Of whom does the meeting you speak of consist?

T.—The Preachers of the District, and the Trustees, Stewards, and Leaders of the Circuit, each of whom has a single vote, and who have power to remove such Preacher from that Circuit, and suspend him from all public duties till the next Conference. (Plan of Pacification, sec. 2.)

SECTION V.

QUARTERLY MEETINGS.

Pupil.—What is a Quarterly Meeting?

Tutor.—The acknowledged organ of the people, composed of Travelling Preachers, Local Preachers, Leaders, Trustees of Chapels, and Stewards; for the purpose of managing the affairs of the circuit, approving the Preachers' bills, and paying in the moneys subscribed for their support.

P.—I have understood that whilst the discussion of the Preacher's bills is proceeding, his manner is somewhat remarkable.

T.—The whole scene is so humiliating to him that it might naturally be thought sufficient of itself to check every notion of ministerial independence. One could almost weep over the infirmities of human nature, to behold a man immediately after this exhibition of dependence ungratefully assuming the most conceited, petulant, and tyrannical airs imaginable!

P.—What is a Circuit Steward?

T.—A sort of Tithe Receiver or Cashier to the Travelling Preacher.

P.—Is there any difference between a Tithe Meeting in the Church and a Quarterly Meeting of the circuit?

T.—Yes; in the former the clergyman treats his parishioners to a dinner, in the latter the guests treat themselves.

P.—Is there no other difference?

T.—In the former, the individuals are laymen; in the latter, they participate in the pastoral and spiritual character of the Minister.

P.—What are the powers of the Quarterly Meeting?

T.—It is invested with the whole management of the temporal concerns of the Travelling Preachers.

P.—Has it any other jurisdiction?

T.—Yes; it has power to try an accused Preacher, all the Preachers in the district being present, and every member of the meeting being entitled to vote, the verdict being found by the majority. (See Plan of Pacification concerning Discipline.)

P.—What other matters are committed to the Quarterly Meeting?

T.—All matters belonging to the circuit; as to the Leaders' Meeting are committed all matters belonging to the Society. (See Concessions, section 4.)

P.—Have the privileges of the Quarterly Meeting ever been invaded by the Conference or their agents?

T.—Yes; in many instances: they were shamelessly trampled on by the forcible introduction of organs into Brunswick Chapel, Liverpool; Grosvenor-street Chapel, Manchester; and Brunswick Chapel, Leeds, but particularly the last of these places.

P.—What were the principal features of the Leeds case?

T.—1. There existed a clear understanding with some of the subscribers to the erection of the chapel, that no organ was to be introduced. 2. In the face of this, the Trustees, (who are in many cases not even members of Society,) brought forward a proposal to set up an organ. 3. A motion to that effect was proposed in the Leaders' Meeting, and rejected. 4. The motion was then brought forward again in the District Meeting, and rejected. 5. The privileges of the Leaders' Meeting were contemned by the refusal to submit to its decision, as were those of the Quarterly Meeting, by carrying the motion over its head into the District Meeting. 6. In spite of all this manifest public disapprobation, the Conference sent down their authority for the immediate erection of the organ.

P.—Do not the Conference justify themselves by saying the case was an extraordinary one?

T.—That it was a *most* extraordinary one none will dispute; such a transaction is not perhaps registered in the page of history. Now, inasmuch as the law says that all matters belonging to a Society are committed to the Leaders' Meeting, and all matters belonging to a circuit are committed to a Quarterly Meeting, and the Conference did, in contradiction to the one, and in contempt of the other, by their own simple fiat, cause an organ to be erected (a matter belonging both to the Society and the circuit,) the Conference have brought themselves into this discreditable dilemma; they have either acted contrary to law, (which makes their conduct illegal and criminal,) or they have acted above the law, (which proves them to be arbitrary, despotic, and absolute.) In the former case, they are guilty before the Methodist public, who have a right to demand satisfaction; and in the latter case, if they assert that they have a right to supersede all law in extraordinary cases, this is the very insult which Englishmen cannot brook; the state of things which has produced all the mischiefs complained of, and the very grievance which the Association is resolved to have redressed.

P.—Did the people submit?

T.—No; they resolutely opposed the insolent and unconstitutional proceeding.

P.—And what followed?

T.—A thousand persons were driven from the Society.

P.—Does it appear that the Conference is more concerned for *organs* or *for the loss of souls?*

T.—For organs, evidently.

P.—But what says the Scripture?

T.—"It must needs be that offences come, but woe to him by whom the offence cometh."

P.—Does not a recent biographer of Mr. Watson pass some singular observations on this Leeds case?

T.—Most imprudently he has done so, in that part of his work in which it became his duty to remark upon Mr. Watson's celebrated defence of these extraordinary proceedings of Conference. A candid historian, as he might readily have shown that Mr. Watson was both a great and good man, would unhesitatingly have noticed this false step, as the principal, perhaps the only blot upon his memory.

P.—Will not the manner in which the said biographer has stated the facts of the Leeds case materially affect the credit of his book in other particulars?

T.—Most materially; and it renders another biography of that great man indispensably necessary. It must also throw considerable discredit upon the authority of certain statements the biographer may advance in the monthly periodical of which he is the editor.

P.—But is there not something extraordinary in the biographer's narrative of the Leeds case?

T.—It presents a singular specimen of that cool impudence which perhaps nothing but habitual delinquency can inspire: never was a more disreputable passage penned by a Minister of the Gospel. To such a tissue of misrepresentation and unfeeling defamation of character, we may surely be allowed to apply the epithet "unprincipled." Thank God, however, the judgment of this unpardonable case is at length likely to be taken out of the hands of Holy Inquisitors, and to be pronounced by an impartial Christian public.

P.—Did he not attempt to weave again the cobweb sophistry of his *protegé*?

T.—He did; but he had presumed the interest of the subject to have died away.

P.—Is not the sophistry peculiarly founded?

T.—It is founded, in the first instance, in falsehood,

as to the characters of the much-wronged victims of Conference cruelty ; and, secondly, on some mystified inferences drawn from the distinction between Independent Churches and a Connexion ; upon which it need only be observed, that, whether as Methodists we exist in the character of Independent Churches, or as a Connexion, or are even guilty of " low dissent," it is still ludicrous effrontery indeed for those to set up themselves as sole patentees of an inherent and Divine right, who have manifested such an extraordinary propensity to do wrong.

P.—Has it not been pronounced unfair for an historian or biographer in this way to interweave a disputed point with his story ?

T.—Yes; the passage is a most cowardly attack upon the character of the Leeds *Protestants;* it is a sort of waylaying the reader, and resembles, in its malignity, though not in its ability, Mr. Gibbon's insidious attacks upon Christianity. As to the peaceable and satisfied state of the Leeds people since 1827, some light may perhaps be thrown on that subject by the steps they may now take when an opportunity of redress presents itself.

P.—Have not the rights of the Quarterly Meeting been infringed by the Conference in the case of the *Theological Institution ?*

T.—That must not be forgotten, certainly : the transactions in regard to the College have been singularly marked by Conference infatuation and contempt of the Methodist public.

P.—Please to explain this.

T.—Was it not contempt of the people's rights to propose such an institution without consulting the constituted authorities in Methodism ? and was it not presumption, nay, madness, to expect that the

people would allow the matter to proceed under such circumstances?

P.—It would seem, then, by the disrespect shown to the official members of the Quarterly Meetings, that they are to be regarded as mere ciphers in the Church?

T.—Precisely so; said a *Reverend* Gentleman on a memorable occasion in Liverpool.

P.—But do not the Preachers say that the subscriptions to the college are to be *voluntary?*

T.—How can that be, when the Missionary fund, and the Contingent fund, subscribed by *all the people*, are to contribute towards it? Not to mention that Dr. Bunting's services as President are to be devoted to it, against the laws of the Missionary Society, which require his exclusive attention as Missionary Secretary!

P.—But what constituted authorities have the Conference contemned by this measure?

T.—The authority of the Quarterly Meeting.

P.—In what way?

T.—No new rule of any Conference can be enforced in a circuit, the Quarterly Meeting of which has objected thereto, until the ensuing Conference. (Concessions, sec. 7.)

P.—But what have the circuits to do with the college?

T.—What have the *circuits* to do with it! What has any one else to do with it? And do not the Preachers themselves say it was only projected to please the people?

P.—Have the Conference then not allowed their rule on the subject to hang in suspense the legal twelve months, in order to afford an opportunity to the Quarterly Meetings to discuss the matter?

T.—No; the law for the establishment of the college was only passed this year, and now every kind of arrangement (except merely the getting of the needful from the people) is made for bringing it into immediate operation.

P.—But has the subject ever been introduced into the Quarterly Meetings ?

T.—There we are again. It would appear that the Preachers have received peremptory orders from some quarter to suspend all official conversation, and at the peril of their ministerial existence to put no motion on the question.

P.—Are you certain of that ?

T.—I refer you to those who have attempted to bring the matter forward in such meetings.

P.—And what is the consequence ?

T.—Why, of course, without the Preacher's consent no measure of a Quarterly Meeting, according to law, is valid.

P.—But do you suspect that the Conference of Methodist Preachers would condescend to such a piece of chicanery as that ?

T.—I leave others to decide that point.

P.—You have just said that the preachers declare the measure to have been brought forward to please the people ?

T.—I did : but you forget that the term people is used in different senses by different persons ; just as when a moralist, speaking of a *good* man, means a *virtuous* man, at the same time that a merchant would understand thereby a *substantial* or *monied* man.

P.—How do you apply the analogy to the present case ?

T.—Merely to show that by the term people, in this connexion, is meant the "influential," or *monied* folks among us.

P.—Is it a fact, then, that organs, colleges, and such like things have immolated, as with the sacrificial knife, so many precious souls, to please so inconsiderable a party as the aristocracy of Methodism !

T.—It is much to be feared that is precisely the case.   And it is conjectured, as an inference from all these circumstances, that under an ostensibly good appearance, the College is only intended to be a sort of propaganda of the unconstitutional and worldly policy of the dominant party in Conference.

P.—Has it not been surmised that it is the intention of Conference to have an organ and the liturgy introduced into every Methodist chapel ?

T.—It is probable that is their design ultimately.

P.—Have not some rumours also been afloat that there are soon to be Methodist Prelates and Bishoprics?

T.—Things do indeed seem to verge rapidly to that consummation ; and by and by we may have a Convocation instead of the Conference, consisting, perhaps, of Bps. Grindrod, Newton, Lessey, Jackson, Crowther, Cubitt, Anderson, Wood, Scott, Ward, and some twenty others, with the newly-created Doctor of Divinity at the head, as Methodist Primate of all England.

P.—Is there not recorded somewhere a remarkable sentiment expressed in connexion with the Leeds business by the said D.D. ?

T.—There is; it was to the effect that the Archbishop of Canterbury did not possess any thing like the power of the President of Conference: so that besides a Convocation, the Christian world is likely to be favoured with a Methodist edition of the Grand Inquisitor, and the Supreme Court of the Holy Inquisition.

P.—Are there not Leaders and Local Preachers in the Quarterly Meetings, who are indifferent to the

ts and signs of the times? nay, who even oppose
y attempt to reform the abuses you have de-
ed?

—Strange to say! it is so.   But "they know
what they do."   They have not yet seen it to be
 duty to oppose a Conference measure.   They
, however, not long hence.

—And what then?

—They are now preparing the fetters they will
be obliged to wear; and, too late, will discover
fatally they have been the dupes of others.

—Is not their supineness under such circum-
es greatly to be blamed?

—Yes; and I say, more than that, when "the
enters into their own souls," let no man pity
!

—You are a little too warm, I fear.

—No: their punishment is just, for by their ill-
ed opposition they betray their Brethren and the
s of the people, which, as the people's repre-
tives, they are bound sacredly to maintain.

—The law requires the presence and sanction of
uperintendent Preacher to render valid a resolu-
of the Quarterly, or Leaders' Meeting.   If the
rintendent then think proper to leave the chair,
not this, in all cases, render the proceedings of
meeting during his absence illegal?

—If it be clear that the Superintendent, in
ng the chair, does so from party and interested
es, in order to frustrate a legal measure brought
rd by the Brethren in such meeting, although
Superintendent act under the shadow of law, in
y, the meeting is a constitutional and proper
vithout him.

—But will the Conference receive an address

from the people when the Superintendent has so refused his sanction?

T.—Certainly not; because they themselves are in the intrigue, and the Superintendent is all the while acting as their agent, and by their command.

P.—Are they not justified in such refusal by the law?

T.—By the letter of the law they may be, but the spirit of the law is obviously evaded by a mere trick, equally inconsistent with the character of a gentleman and a Christian.

P.—May not the Conference interpretation of the law in this case still be the proper one?

T.—If so, the Conference, when drawing up the laws, were guilty of a most discreditable breach of faith with the people, by telling them, as we have seen, that the greatest part of the executive government had been given up to them, when, in fact, the whole transaction was a piece of collusion, by which the Quarterly and Leader's Meetings were left at the mercy of any capricious or interested Superintendent, and as much under the power of Conference as before.

P.—Then you presume your construction of the law to be the true one?

T.—Most certainly; because to deny it, is directly to bring home to the Conference the charge of cunning and duplicity, either in the ancient enactment, or in the modern evasion, of the law.

P.—What influence ought *wealth* to have in the proceedings of the Quarterly, Leaders', and other Meetings of the Church?

T.—None at all; any more than in a Court of Justice.

P.—Why?